Level
# 2

# The Nature Kid's Guide to
# RINGTAILS

# DAVID ANDERSON

LP Media Inc. Publishing
Text copyright © 2026 by LP Media Inc.


For information address LP Media Inc. Publishing,
30012 Variolite St NW, Princeton MN 55371
www.lpmedia.org

Publication Data

Ringtails
The Nature Kid's Guide to Ringtails — First edition.

Summary: "Learn all about Ringtails, the Nature Kid Way"
— Provided by publisher.

ISBN: 979-8-89818-260-1

[1. Ringtails – Non-Fiction] I. Title.

Title: The Nature Kid's Guide to Ringtails

# CONTENTS

# ROCKY REALMS

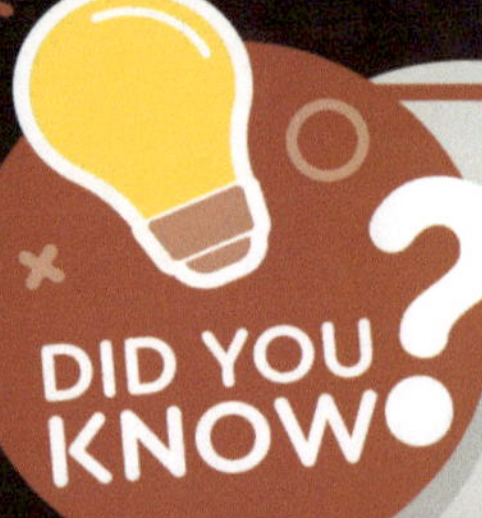



Long ago, miners kept ringtails as pets to catch mice — they called them 'miner's cats'!

**Skitter! A ringtail scrambles up a dark canyon wall.**

Something moves in the darkness between the canyon rocks. It has enormous eyes, radar-dish ears, and a tail striped like a raccoon. Most people have never seen one — but the ringtail has been watching them for years.

Ringtails are expert hiders. They tuck into rock cracks, caves, and hollow logs during the day and come alive at night. Cliffs and canyons are their **territory**.

Small, quick, and almost impossibly hard to spot, the ringtail is one of North America's best kept wild secrets.

# DESERT DWELLERS

Ringtails can live from the low desert floor to snowy mountain tops at 9,000 feet!

**Whoosh! A dry desert wind blows sand past a resting ringtail.**

Ringtails are found across a huge stretch of western North America, from the forests of Oregon all the way down to the dry hills of southern Mexico.

Most of them prefer warm, rocky country. Deserts, dry canyons, and rugged hillsides are their sweet spot. But some live near streams or in forests, proving these animals are more flexible than most people realize.

Texas, Arizona, and California are ringtail hotspots. All three states have exactly what a ringtail needs — rocks, warmth, and plenty of places to disappear.

# SMALL STUFF

FUN
FACT!
A ringtail's body is about the
size of a large squirrel, but its
tail makes it look twice as big!

**Squeak! A tiny ringtail peeks out from behind a stone.**

Ringtails are about the size of a small cat. Their bodies are 12 to 14 inches long — barely longer than a ruler!

But their fluffy tails add a lot more length. From nose to tail tip, a ringtail stretches over two feet long. The tail alone can be just as long as the body!

Even so, ringtails are very light. They weigh only about two pounds. You could easily hold one in your two hands.

RAD RINGS

## Swish! A ringtail waves its long, striped tail at dusk.

The best part of a ringtail is its tail! It has 14 to 16 black and white rings. The bushy tail waves like a flag in the dark.

Soft, tan fur covers a ringtail's back. Its belly is creamy white. Dark fur circles each big eye, just like a mask.

Ringtails have pointed noses and flat faces. Some people say they look like a mix of a cat and a fox!

Some people call ringtails 'civet cats' — but they are not cats at all!

# NIGHT EYES

FUN FACT!

A ringtail's eyes glow bright green when a light shines on them at night!

**Creak! A ringtail hears a mouse step on a dry twig.**

Ringtails are made for the dark. Their huge eyes let in lots of light, helping them see well when they hunt at night. Those big eyes take up most of their face!

Big, round ears pick up every tiny sound. A ringtail can hear a mouse move in the leaves. It can even hear bugs crawl across a rock.

Long whiskers help, too. They feel the shape of tight spaces. This comes in handy when a ringtail slips between rocks.

STINK
SPRAY

## Pssst! A ringtail sprays a stinky mist from under its tail.

When a ringtail feels trapped, it has a stinky trick. It can spray a bad smell from **glands** under its tail. The awful stink keeps enemies away.

Ringtails also bark and hiss when danger is near. They puff up their bushy tails to look bigger and scarier.

Most of the time, ringtails just run and hide. But the stink spray helps when they have no other choice. It is their secret weapon!

A scared ringtail can scream so loud you can hear it from a quarter mile away!

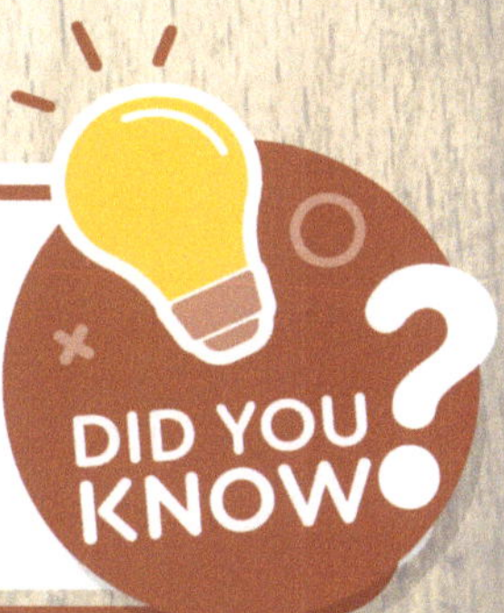

# MUNCHY MENU

DID YOU KNOW?
In fall, ringtails stuff themselves with extra fruit and bugs to build up fat for winter!

## Crunch! A hungry ringtail bites into a big, juicy beetle.

Ringtails eat many kinds of food. They munch on bugs like beetles, crickets, and moths. Insects are their favorite snack!

Fruit and berries are yummy treats, too. Ringtails also eat mice, lizards, and small birds. They can even gobble up spiders and scorpions without getting hurt!

A ringtail is not a picky eater. It will eat whatever it can find, which helps it survive in places where food is hard to find.

# SNEAK SNACKS

**Snap! A ringtail sees a mouse move in the bushes and jumps to catch it.**

Ringtails are sneaky hunters. They creep slowly and stay low to the ground. When they spot a bug or mouse, they pounce fast!

Speed helps a lot. A ringtail can grab a moth right out of the air. Its sharp claws pin down prey in a flash.

Ringtails hunt alone each night. They search under rocks, in bushes, and along creek beds. Nothing is safe from a hungry ringtail on the prowl.

WATCH OUT
DID YOU KNOW?
A great horned owl can spot a ringtail moving in nearly total darkness from 100 feet away!
20

## Whooo! An owl swoops toward a ringtail on a branch.

Life for a ringtail means staying one step ahead of danger at all times. Great horned owls are the biggest threat from above — silent, fast, and nearly impossible to hear coming.

On the ground, the list grows longer. Coyotes, bobcats, and foxes all hunt ringtails. Even large snakes will take one if they get the chance.

Young ringtails face the greatest risk of all. Small, slow, and still learning the rules of survival, they stay tucked deep inside their dens until they are ready to face the world.

QUICK
CLIMB

## Zip! A ringtail shoots up a steep cliff to escape a fox.

When danger comes, a ringtail moves fast. It can scramble up a steep cliff in seconds. Its claws dig into tiny cracks in the rock.

If it cannot climb, it hides. A ringtail can squeeze into a hole just two inches wide! Most predators are too big to follow.

Ringtails also freeze and stay very still. Their tan fur blends in with the rocks around them, making them almost invisible.

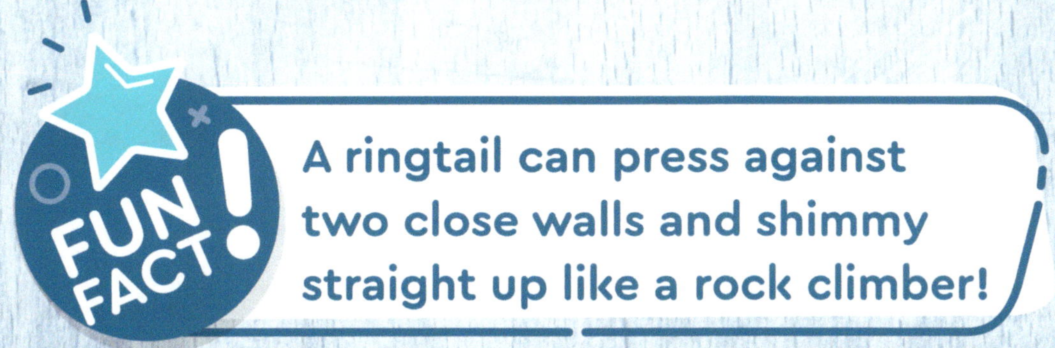


A ringtail can press against two close walls and shimmy straight up like a rock climber!

# AGILE ACROBATS

## Flip! A ringtail spins around on a branch and races away.

Ringtails are some of the best climbers around. Their back ankles can spin all the way around — a full 180 degrees! This lets them climb down trees and cliffs headfirst.

They walk along thin branches with ease. Their long tails swing from side to side to keep them steady. It is like watching a circus act!

Ringtails can run fast on the ground, too. They twist and turn to dodge rocks and bushes. Nothing slows these acrobats down!

# NIGHT SHIFT

DID YOU KNOW?
Ringtails may use a different sleeping spot almost every night to stay safe from predators!

## Rustle! A ringtail wakes up as the sun begins to set.

Ringtails are **nocturnal**, which means they sleep through the entire day tucked inside a rocky den or hollow tree. When darkness falls, they stretch, shake off sleep, and head out.

Night is when ringtails come alive. They spend hours hunting for food, patrolling their territory, and learning every rock and trail in their home range. In between, they take time to groom their fur, cleaning it carefully the way a cat does.

Before sunrise, they slip back into their dens. The day belongs to others — the night belongs to the ringtail.

# LONE RANGERS

A male ringtail may roam across an area bigger than 100 football fields — about 136 acres!

## Scratch! A lone ringtail slips through the quiet canyon.

Ringtails like to be alone. They do not live in groups or packs. Each one has its own space to roam.

A ringtail marks its area with scent. This tells other ringtails to stay out! Males and females only meet up during mating time.

Ringtails spend most of their lives on their own. Being solo helps each one find enough food. Less sharing means more eating!

SPRING
SONGS

## Chirp! A ringtail calls out to find a mate on a spring evening.

In spring, ringtails look for mates. Males make high chirping sounds to call to females. A male may travel far to find one.

When a female is ready, the male stays near. They touch noses and clean each other's fur. This pair stays together for just a short while.

After mating, the pair splits up. The male heads back to his own area. They may not meet again until the next spring.

**A female ringtail is only ready to mate for about one single day each year!**

TINY TOTS
DID YOU KNOW?
A newborn ringtail weighs less than one ounce — lighter than a slice of bread!
32

**Squeak! A ringtail kit wiggles inside its warm, dark den.**

Baby ringtails are born in late spring or early summer. A mother usually has two to four babies at a time. The tiny babies are called kits.

Newborn kits are very small — only about four inches long. Their eyes are shut and their ears are closed. They have thin, fuzzy fur and cannot see or hear a thing.

The kits drink their mother's milk and grow fast. In about four weeks, their eyes finally open wide. Then they start to peek at the world around them.

MOM
KNOWS

**Chitter! A mother ringtail nuzzles her tiny kits in the den.**

Mother ringtails do all the work of raising their kits. They keep the babies warm and feed them milk. The den stays cozy and safe.

As the kits grow, their mother brings them bits of solid food. She shows them how to eat bugs and fruit. The kits watch her closely and learn.

By fall, the young ringtails are ready to go. They leave the den to find their own territory. Mom's job is done — until next spring!

A mother ringtail moves her kits to a new den right away if she senses any danger!

# SUPER SURVIVORS

## Drip! A ringtail licks water from a crack in the rocks.

Ringtails are tough little survivors. They can find food and water in very dry places. Their bodies do not need much water to keep going.

On hot days, they stay cool in their shady dens. On cold nights, they fluff their thick fur for warmth. They can handle big swings in temperature — from freezing cold to blazing hot.

People can help ringtails by keeping wild lands safe. Leaving rocks and old trees alone gives ringtails places to live and hide.

# SPOT THEM

Rangers at the Grand Canyon often see ringtails sneaking around the lodges at night looking for snacks!

## Click! A flashlight beam finds two glowing eyes in the dark.

Want to see a ringtail? Head to a rocky desert canyon after dark and bring a dim red light — ringtails are far less spooked by red light than bright white, giving you a much better chance of a real sighting.

Scan the ledges and tree branches slowly. Watch for two tiny eyes reflecting back at you. Listen for soft scratching sounds on rock.

Patience is everything. Ringtails are shy, elusive, and rarely seen even by people who spend time in their habitat. Spotting one is a genuine wild moment — the kind most people never get.

# GLOSSARY

### nocturnal
Active at night and sleeping during the day

### territory
An area an animal claims and defends as its own

### den
A safe hiding place where an animal rests

### gland
A small organ inside the body that makes and releases a liquid

### elusive
Very hard to find or spot, even when you are looking